BRIGHT

BUSINESS

IDEAS

D1016127

Brian Lovig

First Printing June, 1993

ISBN 0-9697150-0-5

Published and Distributed by

Bright Publishing Inc.
Box 24002, Downtown P.O.
Kelowna, British Columbia
Canada V1Y 9P9

Bright Publishing Inc.
Room 261, Box 5000
Oroville, Washington
U.S.A. 98844

Published Simultaneously in
Canada and
the United States of America

Printed in Canada

Contents   Page No.

Contents

About the Author

Brian Lovig, born and raised on the prairies, now lives in the Okanagan Valley, British Columbia, north of Washington State.

At an early age and with little formal education Brian began a career in the auctioneering business. He has never restricted himself from exploring any avenue of business or from trying any venture. Along the way he has enjoyed many successes and gained valuable and practical business experience from each situation.

From creating names for new food products, trademarking and selling them to multi-national corporations, to buying and selling large tracts of land, apartment complexes and high-rise buildings, Brian has tried it all!

His uncanny ability to come up with new concepts for development and novel ideas for marketing, has brought many people seeking assistance or guidance in sales and creativity, to his door.

Realizing that he had more bright business ideas than he could ever practically do on his own, he came up with the best concept of all – to publish some of his ideas in a book.

Bright Business Ideas. Truly a recipe book for creativity and business! Read on and you will discover more kinds of ideas than you ever imagined. Try the Ski Locker idea as a first-ever business venture or incorporate Storeboards as a new national division within an existing corporation.

A bright business idea is like the concrete foundation of a tall building. If it is solid and constructed properly, it will be sturdy and long lasting.

A proper business plan and its implementation are important. Investigate all legal aspects and regulations pertaining to any Bright Business Idea taken from this book.

Switching concepts, adding and deleting items from any idea can enhance it. Changes reflect input and custom-form the idea for its user. For example, Sports Banners can be designed in various shapes, called by another name, and even marketed in one city, county or country. Use them as shown or use your imagination to build on the original idea.

The future belongs to those who question the present, those who do not hesitate to challenge established ideas, and those who pursue bright ideas of their own.

Happy business!

Brian Lovig

Sports Banners

Wave a banner! A brand new fun idea!

Product:
A Sports Banner is like a scarf; approximately four feet long, six to eight inches wide and has messages screened or placed on it. Banners can be made from acetate or nylon fabric. Sports Banners will cause great excitement at a sports event! The banners need to be in team colors and display a team logo at each end. Alternate messages can be put on the banners if desired. Fans would wear or wave the banners or knot them together to make "team bands."

Market:
All sports events including professional basketball, football, baseball and hockey. . . college, minor league and junior teams in all events make up an extremely large market. Thousands of fans are encouraging sports teams every day. In addition, Sports Banners can be promoted for use at concerts and political rallies.

Marketing and
Distribution Plan:
• Sell via conventional outlets such as sporting goods stores, drug stores, discount stores and in arena or stadium concessions.

(Continued on page 12)

• Sell before or during an event.

• Sell advertising to a sponsor and distribute Sports Banners free or at a reduced charge. For example, if a cola company was the advertiser on Sports Banners and the banners were given away to fans at no charge, the cola company would stand to benefit through increased use of its product. The stadium would likely feel obligated to carry the cola company's product. The cola name and logo would be in front of every fan, close up, and would be picked up by television and other media to an extent determined by the size and strength of the sports event and league. More than one advertiser could appear on a banner. Potential advertisers include automotive dealerships, food stores, sports stores and beverage companies.

Potential:
The cost of manufacturing Sports Banners may vary from one geographic region to another as may the suggested retail price. The Sports Banner concept could command a profit in any area and at virtually all sports events. If done nationally with a professional sports league, this idea has the potential of earning millions of dollars.

This concept has high scoring potential for fun and profit!

Possible Names: Sports Banners
Sports Scarf
Cheerbanner

BBQ Pit Stop

Something new from something old!

Use a mobile BBQ cart like those used in many cities to sell hot dogs and pretzels. This concept involves selling large volumes of product that will be taken home for use.

For example, a chicken franchise. . . without the real estate and other overhead costs! The plan would be to BBQ items like ribs & chicken and to sell them in buckets or similar containers.

A good location for the cart is important. Make a sign for the cart which indicates the quality of food, ie.: purchased at "well known supermarket" (gives credibility); its BBQ flavor, its price and its take home convenience. "Buy now, re-heat at home" is an appropriate suggestion.

Possible Names: Colonel Cart
                         BBQ A La Cart

Funny Money

I did so badly last year that I didn't have to borrow to pay my taxes.

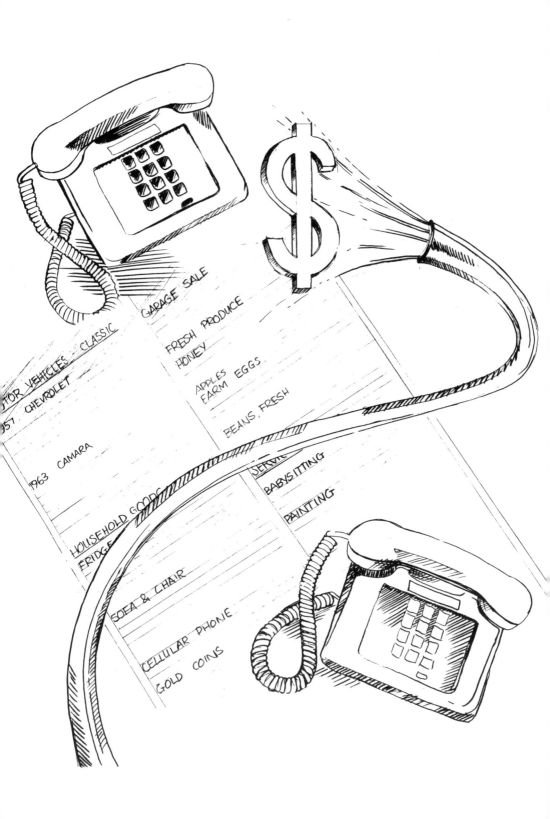

Flea Market Phone Idea

Obtain a 1-900 telephone number (user-pay service) by which you match buyers and sellers of merchandise. Run an ad in the newspaper, ie.: "If you want to sell or buy. . . anything! T.V.'s, radios, beds or a car, phone now." When a caller wants to sell a radio, you list the item in the sales system. When a caller is interested in buying a radio, you list that information in the buy system. Then you connect the two of them and they negotiate or complete their own deal. You get paid directly from the phone company for the time that both the buyer and seller spent on the pay-to-use phone system.

To encourage buyer activity in some markets, consider providing the no-charge 1-800 telephone service for buyers.

Flea Market Management

Create an indoor or outdoor mall. . . Secure a location and prepare a package to show what promotion and other services you will provide. Solicit those who regularly display merchandise at flea markets to locate to your new facility. Your revenue will come from stall, table and accessory rentals and from admissions.

Concept: To design and develop a chain of restaurants and bars which relate directly to the business of real estate.

Market: Realtors form the main target market for this idea. The market is assured as realtors can also be involved in the initial funding of the locations.

There are approximately 1.1 million realtors in North America and many, many others who are involved directly or indirectly in the real estate industry. These include real estate developers, entrepreneurs and financiers.

Design: The interior design should include photos, prints, and items relating to this industry. An example would be newspaper clippings of various transactions of Howard Hughes, the Empire State Building "flip" and other well known real estate deals. Local news coverage can also be used, ie.: "Best Salesman Award" or "Local landmark purchased by a certain group."

Monopoly board design table cloths would be a neat decor idea.

(Continued on next page)

Menu: Examples for the menu are:

- "High-rise" (club-house sandwich)
- "Single Family" (single burger)
- "Duplex" (open faced sandwich)
- "Raw Land" (veggie platter)
- "Walk-up" (double burger)
- "Sales Commission" (glass of water)
- "Prime Property" (prime rib)
- "Foreclosure"
    (a type of drink from the bar)
- "High Interest" (bourbon)
- "Flips" (pancakes)
- "Turnovers" (apple pie)

Funding: Realtors are targeted for the raising of the funds. There are approximately 100,000 realtors in Canada and 1,000,000 in the United States.

Funding
Possibilities:

- Pre-sale of services, ie.: sell a $1,200.00 food and beverage credit for $1,000.00.
- Memberships.
- Public shares by prospectus.
- Public Shares by private placement.
- Limited partnership.
- Loans from realtors; make regular payments on the principal and the interest could be repaid in food or drink credits.

Note:

Many lenders will advance $1,000.00 or more on pre-approved personal credit. This package allows for a controlled sales presentation and no cash outlay for the customer.

An example for a first unit start-up: Arrange for $1,000.00 personal loans from a local bank (on approved credit); attend sales meetings at real estate companies where dozens of people will attend at one time, and sell up to 200 units at $1,000.00 each. Retain a reasonable fee, borrow some additional money if required and construct the facilities. Several variations of this example are feasible.

Management Plan:

Incorporate a new company if required. Prepare a business plan and arrange for funds required for the start-up program. Employ a president or manager for the company. His or her job is to select an area for the first location, complete graphic designs and sales literature, raise the money required from the local real estate people, oversee construction and supervise the operation of the business.

(Continued on page 23)

21

The president is responsible for rolling out the concept to all major centers.

When in operation, the business clientele will be strong and consistent since they funded the operations. They now have locations across town and across the country in which to meet with their peers and establish their networks.

Possible Names: Dealers
Real Estate Club
Challenge Club

How can I be overdrawn? I still have checks/cheques.

Airline In-Plane Advertising

Here's a high flying idea!

Millions of air travellers daily stare at the back of the seat in front of them. These seat backs hold the fold-down tray used for lunches. Contract the space on each side of the trays from the airline companies to sell advertising space. The best way to buy the tray space is by way of a percentage split of sales or income with the airline company.

What a way to capture the attention of the consumers! They have to stare at the message for hours. Potential advertisers include car rental firms (by the time travellers exit the plane through the terminal they will certainly recognize the name!), hotels, travel agents, stores, perfumes, gifts and magazines. The potential for profit is enormous. Most airlines would also enjoy the supplement to their incomes.

A good name for this new medium is "Fly Boards."

Money talks. . . mine just stutters.

Business Barber

A cut above the rest!

Business people today are often short of time and many would gladly pay for a barber or hairstylist to come to their homes or businesses. No more waiting in a line for a haircut or missed appointments. Clients will now have their personal stylist and finally be able to have regular haircuts.

Prepare a brochure, complete with photos and mail drop them to potential clients. Personal contact is also recommended.

This is a great idea for an individual or business to organize, hire barbers (several) and secure clients.

When you can't change the direction of the wind. . . adjust your sails.

An old news idea!

Prepare histories of houses. Assemble the information into an organized package (with photos if possible) and sell it to the present property owners. Home history is interesting. Who built the house? When? Why? For how much money? What were the names of the former owners or inhabitants? What is their background? For old, old houses, a chart showing sale prices reaching far back would be interesting and entertaining. Research city records, local and other government archives etc. and conduct personal interviews. Any information on the quality of the original construction or on building plans would be useful.

When completed, document the steps and structure used in creating the program. This is now ready for expansion by either employing staff or franchising. There are many old houses in each community with interesting histories and if a few hundred dollars can be earned by preparing a history for one, then the potential is great!

He's been spending money like water and now needs to float a loan.

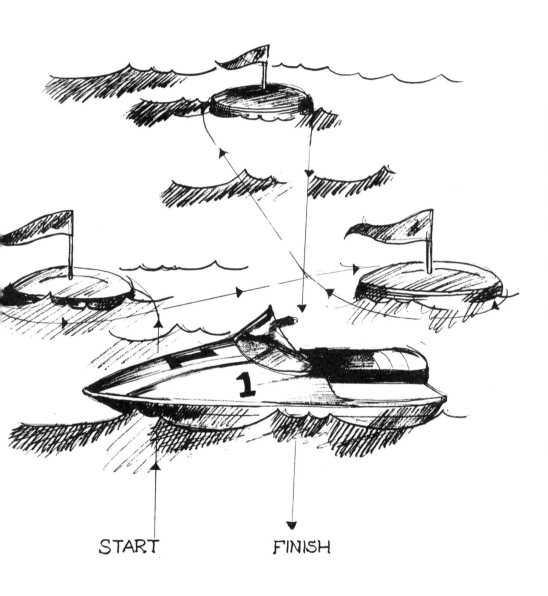

START   FINISH

This idea makes waves!

Lease or rent a suitable water area on a lake. Place three floating barrels strategically in the water in the same design as that of a western rodeo. Design and promote organized races. The best time determines the winner. Offer prize money and awards. The press will love it!

Obtain fees from participants and possibly, from the spectators. Operate or sub-lease a concession stand. Organize more barrel clubs in other areas for competition and recognition of the sport. Approach local marine dealerships for sponsorship of the event (ie.: signs, barrels, flags). This will provide some or all of the funds needed for the start-up costs. Participants should also seek sponsors to reduce their costs and to promote the enterprise of their sponsor.

A monthly fee or a membership fee could be charged to participants. Encourage them to practice the event and to use the facilities.

An appropriate name for sea machine riders is "Water Cowboys."

One who has income pays income tax. The outcome is no income.

Sand Holder

Sand bags have long been used for weight in rear wheel drive automobiles to allow for easier handling. Most often sand bags are purchased at service stations or hardware stores.

The burlap or twine bags are expensive and last only a short time before becoming damp, deteriorating and breaking apart. They are heavy, dirty and messy, making them a nuisance to move and replace.

Design a good plastic holder that will fit in car trunks and truck boxes. A long and narrow fit is best. Particular designs may require anchoring or securing to the vehicle. Then, name it, fill it and sell it!

Possible Names: Mr. Sandman
                    Sandmaster

If nobody sells, a terrible thing happens. . . nothing.

Ski Hill T-Bar

Even at ski villages, advertisers can find great places for messages. For example, the hand bar on the T-bar.

The circumference of the bar is best suited to well-known products like beverages or snack items. Obtain the advertising rights from the ski hill, prepare statistics, set pricing and then, approach advertisers.

Ski Hill Chair Lift

Ski lifts travel to the top of the hill thousands of times per month carrying skiers. The back of each chair lift is a potential location for advertised messages. These are seen by the skiers in the next chair lift. Here is a captive and captivated audience!

Obtain the advertising rights from the ski hill management, prepare statistics and pricing and then, approach prospective clients.

Barter

This is an age old and proven sales method. Barter is best done by independent middle persons because they are better able to contribute the time and effort needed for a concentrated marketing program.

Prepare a brochure and contracts before soliciting potential clients. Arrange for businesses to exchange goods or services they produce or sell for items from other businesses. Charge a cash fee based on a percentage of the value of the trades. This fee can be up to 10% and often be charged from both sides in the transaction. The advantages for the businesses include increased sales and higher profits.

Example: Radio Station   Car Dealer
            (air time)   (automobiles)

Assume each company's barter item has a retail value of $10,000.00. Each has a need for the other's merchandise. The effective cost to each is less than the advertised one indicated because these items are purchased at wholesale prices. This results in a real savings for each firm.

Approach all types of businesses and source the products that they require. Then approach other businesses that have a need for these products or services. Often bartering will work through several companies before the products are permanently exchanged.

The barter company will have to bank or inventory barter items. For example, $10,000.00 of radio air time may be bartered to five businesses for their products; one of chairs, one of coffee supplies, one of newspaper advertising, etc. In this case, the radio station commits to the barter conditionally on approval of the items on the other side of the barter.

Possible Names: Barter Business
                    Barter Brokerage
                    Business Barter System
                    Better Barter Business

RESTAURANT CREDIT
$500·00

NEWSPAPER ADVERTISING
$2000·00

VEHICLE SERVICING
$2500·00

TRAVEL AGENT
$3000·00

STATIONERY & OFFICE EQUIPMENT
$2000·00

$10,000·00 RADIO TIME

BARTER BROKER

Hat Styles

Tough to top this idea!

Hats for men should be back in vogue. They are sensible. . . it rains, snows and blows. . . and hats are stylish.

Approach hat manufacturers and present them with a detailed marketing and distribution plan. Obtain samples and credit lines from them. Approach them for co-op advertising money to be used to enhance their brand name.

Display the hats from portable carts which need to be well located and equipped with an umbrella as the best sales days will be those when it rains. The carts can be very economical as well as being mobile.

It's important to sell the trend. The hat can be tossed in as an extra. Hard hitting signs are needed:

Rain, Snow, Wind, Style
"We have it covered!"

Avoid trendy hats and a diverse inventory. Promote business and casualwear hats in both felt and straw.

Re-create a style which has low overhead and large revenues.

Parking Meter Advertising

You can save the city money. Call the mayor!

Buy or lease the meter heads on parking meters and replace the internal mechanism with a flip or rotation gear. The head may have to be replaced with a larger one, depending on present size. Panels can be inserted which will display different advertising messages each hour. A separate attachment could be designed to fit over part of the existing meter head. Messages are observed whenever a meter is "plugged." A business can now buy advertising space on the street of its choice.

There are millions of parking meters!

T-Shirt Sales

This idea has been around for a long time and will likely be around for a lot longer. See a graphic artist. Design an event or an idea. Buy the shirts. Get them silkscreened. Sell them for more than your combined costs. Target groups like school sports teams and running clubs. Do their team logos or slogans. Current events, when done in cartoon styles, are also popular items. This is ideal and profitable for a one person venture and has the potential of being expanded into large areas and employing several people.

To make your T-shirt business unique, accept trade-ins on all purchases. Wash the old T-shirts and sell them by the pound as rags!

Blue Jean Tattoos

We have had the blues for years. The Denim Blues!

With the recent upsurge and increases in skin tattooing, this idea offers a healthy and less permanent option. Tattoo your jeans! Individual tattoo transfers are purchased and once the perfect spot is determined, pressed into the fabric with an iron. Additional tattoos could be purchased and added until ultimately a pair of jeans could be covered in tattoos. Each pair of jeans could sport trendy tattoos; so to change tattoos, just change your jeans! The potential for this idea is in the development of the product and of sales of the individual tattoos but there is also the opportunity to set up a booth in a mall and do the application of the tattoos on-site, for a small fee.

Possible Names: Tatty's Designs
"Blue on Blue Jean Tattoo"
The Blues
Jean Tattoos
J.T.'s

Lottery Club

You can't win if you don't have a ticket!

Organize several individuals to form a club whose purpose is to buy lottery tickets for a pre-determined time (6 months is best).

The cash contribution from each member should be paid monthly to the one selected to buy the tickets. The more members and the higher the contribution equals more buying power! The odds are great!

The profits (and there have to be some) are not to be re-invested but are to be distributed equally among the members at the end of each term. A regular rotation of members for the collection of money and purchases of tickets is suggested.

Toast Lifters

No more hot fingers! Design a prototype using a clothespin and two popsicle sticks. Attach the sticks to the clothespin with glue. Now you are ready to remove toast from the toaster and you are also ready to go to market!

For extra appeal, color or apply printing on them. Sell advertising space to local bakers, dairies or grocery stores for additional income.

Possible names: Toasteez
                    Toast Tweezers

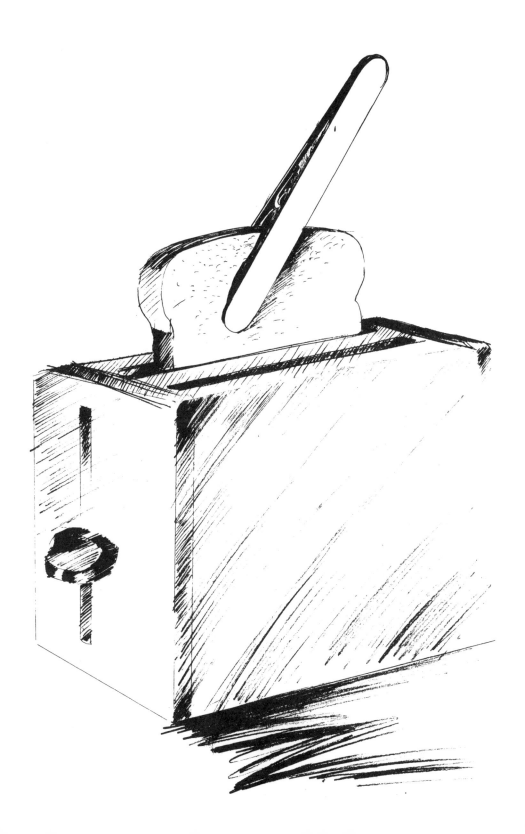

This double use concept is for those who desire a new business challenge or for the professional wanting to expand their business.

Product: Professional services which are available from professional groups. These include law firms, accounting companies, medical doctors, veterinarians and dental clinics.

Market: The market is huge for virtually all groups. For example, the market should include the immediate neighborhood of businesses and individuals. National corporate accounts and government accounts also need to be approached. New arrivals to a city will need a family doctor, lawyer, dentist and accountant. Contact furniture movers, power and telephone companies to obtain names and addresses of new residents.

Marketing Plan: An independent agent, when contracted by the professional group, would conduct extensive research of the group and its people. The agent must learn everything about the product! The agent then contacts potential clients. A retainer or pre-payment for services is a sure way to encourage use. Constant servicing of each account is important. For

(Continued on next page)

best results it is recommended that the agent not have offices with the professional firm and to be an independent agency (not associated with the group). A detailed business plan should be prepared.

Potential: It is expected that this concept could be very profitable for both sides! The agent could be very successful and the professional's business receipts could increase dramatically. These results will vary depending on variables like population and competition.

Conclusion: Few, if any, professionals utilize this method to enhance their business. Someone other than one who performs the service is often best to sell the services. . . professional athletes have agents, so maybe professionals should too.

Success is doing some usual idea and doing it unusually well.

Businesses, farmers and home owners often require money for building, expansion, inventory and equipment. Many have difficulty obtaining financing. Conventional lenders seldom support enterprises and although these types of lenders should be approached for money, other sources need to be found.

Establish a Money Brokerage company. Research laws and regulations pertaining to the operation of this form of business. Solicit clients. Charge an up-front fee, plus a percentage of the amount of money obtained for the client. The up-front fee is important as it forms a commitment for each party. Prepare a detailed and interesting loan package. Include illustrations and financial information. A major source of funds is from the individuals known to the clients. Obtain a list of all of their friends, neighbors and family members. As an independent contractor, the Money Broker is best able to deal in these areas. The lenders also benefit as the interest rates paid can be significantly higher than interest paid on savings. This business can be very rewarding.

Behold the turtle. He makes progress only when he sticks his neck out.

Pay Phone Cleaner

This idea eliminates dirty talk!

Product:
A packaged moist and disposable cloth or a fitted paper cover to be dispensed from a vending machine. Pay phone customers can now avoid odors and germs left from previous callers. Cigarette smoke, perfume and other odors are often present. Callers' mouths also are often in direct contact with the mouth piece of a telephone. The moist cloth can be used to wipe and disinfect the mouth piece of the phone before each use.

Market:
There are tens of millions of pay phones in the world. Many of these are in North America. The number of calls that are made annually from pay phones is incredible!

Marketing Plan:
Locate pre-packaged moist cloths and vending machines. Prepare advertising to place on the vending machine which will explain the health reasons for the user to buy the product. Prepare pricing and costs. Contact the phone companies to obtain space for the vending machines.

(Continued on next page)

For example, arrange for the owner of a restaurant to place a vending machine on the wall beside the pay phone. Arrange for a garbage bin beside the pay phone for the used cloths. Explore the possibility of advertising on the bin for additional revenue.

Conclusion:

Pay phone cleaners are long overdue! However, the public and the telephone companies must be educated as to the value of this idea. The profit potential is enormous! From regional to national. . . from short to long distance!

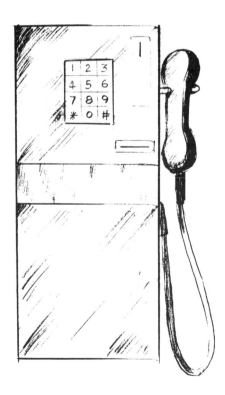

This is a huge market that mysteriously has been ignored.

There are more than 75,000,000 pet dogs and cats in North America alone! There are a few pet cemetery services in some areas and none at all in most. Deceased pets usually end up as fertilizer or some other undesirable commodity. Pets most often effectively become family members. People prefer that deceased dogs and cats be buried properly for peace of mind for themselves and their families.

Pet cemeteries are a necessity in many areas and can be very profitable.

Watch for big problems. They disguise big opportunities.

Petro Vision

This idea is a gas!

Service stations frequently have cardboard or plastic uprights on their gas pumps advertising a limited number of items. These ads are most often services or products of the gas company. The upright is sometimes referred to as a "pump talker." Although they are somewhat effective, there remains that lengthy time span in which customers have little else to attract their attention. This is the case in both a self service or a full service situation.

Computerized screens could replace "pump talkers" and carry advertising images. Moving images would attract the attention of the customer. Because it takes several minutes to fuel a vehicle, the customer is a captive audience. There are approximately 170,000 gas stations in the United States and 18,000 in Canada, the majority of these having two or more gas pumps per retail outlet. The potential is enormous! Although independent studies need to be done for each area, preliminary research shows that Petro Vision would be more effective than radio advertising and that it could be considerably less costly.

Advertisers would be able to specifically target a selected area. Traffic counts and other demographics are readily available. Unlike radio or newspaper promotions, the advertiser would be able to monitor daily the number of people viewing the company message!

(Continued on page 53)

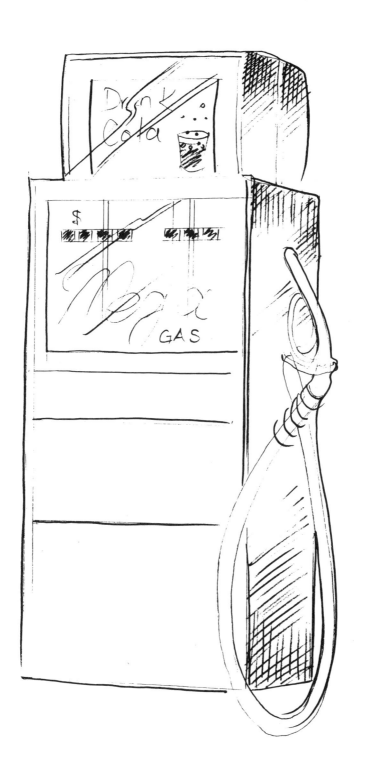

Petro Vision offers an exciting new concept for advertising products and services. Business plans should look at taking the perceived acceptance level of cost to the advertisers and work it back to calculate potential profits. Remember, sooner or later virtually everyone goes to a gas station.

Potential Advertisers
Include:
- Automotive Dealerships

- Snack Foods

- Beverage Companies

- Real Estate Firms

- Grocery Stores

- Auto Accessory Companies

- Motels

Possible Names: Petro Ad
Petro Vision
Pump Talker
Gas Up

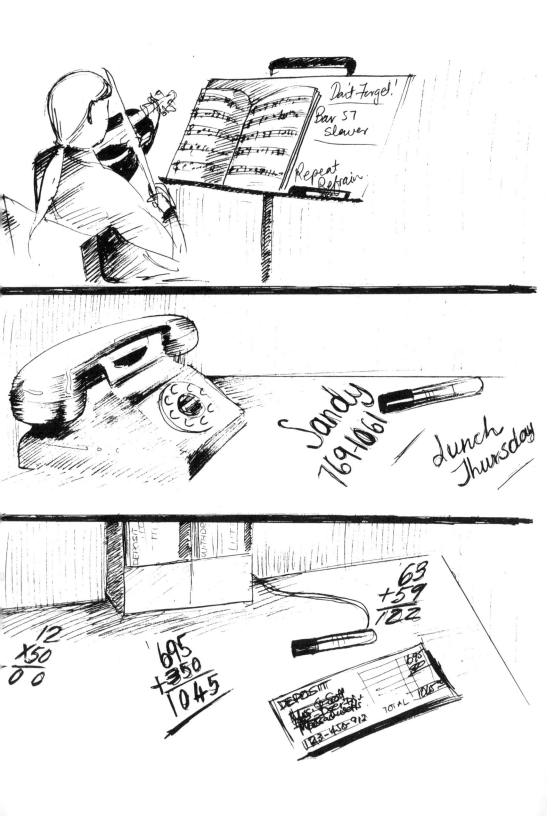

Concept:
Writing boards which are used with felt marking pens are commonly referred to as White Boards. These are easily erased and are becoming increasingly common in homes and offices. Solicit orders for White Boards and custom design them to fit rooms and furniture. For example take an area on a telephone table or the entire top of a desk. Note pads and pencils are often hard to find when needed. Papers having written messages on them are also usually hard to find. White Boards reduce waste, increase efficiency and are neat. White Board material is readily available at lumber yards or office supply centers.

Market:
This is a new but quickly understood idea that fits a huge market. Items include office desks, student desks, residence phone tables, airline desk counters, pay phones, boardroom tables, public washroom walls and restaurant tables.

A market also exists for unattached White Board slates. These could be briefcase size for easy use and mobility.

So many talents! So many good ideas! But how do these ambitious young entrepreneurs get started!?

Here is a great idea for someone who enjoys working with young people and watching them develop their talents, or for a young person with entrepreneurial spirit and organizational skills.

Recruit talented young people with varied abilities. Include the following:
- Artists
- Potters
- Skateboard Enthusiasts
- T-shirt Collectors
- Talented Cooks or Bakers
- Leather Crafters
- Comic and Used Book Collectors
- Clothing Designers
  . . . even someone who enjoys barbecuing!

Then, form a cooperative or a business group with this collection of individuals.

A suitable venue would need to be found for group members to display goods or set up a service. A junior flea market! Members who offer services would always have to be on hand to manage their stalls and those selling goods could take turns promoting their products. Each article would be tagged with the price and the member's name or number in order to keep track of monies owing. A percentage of the revenue would be payable to cover rent, promotions and utilities.

To market. . . to market!

Cattle Idea

Kids and adults would love to start their own "herd" of cattle. Especially city people!

Western folklore and adventure is associated with cattle. Few city dwellers will ever own cattle because of time, financial and space restrictions. The idea is to sell cattle to people who would normally never be associated with this western industry.

Prepare a unique and exciting advertising program. Offer one animal for an amount to be determined after considering costs and expenses.

Present terms for payment and split the profits and calf ownership for your efforts and boarding of the animal. Properly prepared, people everywhere could have the opportunity to be in the cattle business.

Send photos of the animals to their owners. Contribute to the pride of ownership! Enclose details of the ranch where it lives. Keep the owner informed about the appearance and condition of the animal.

This idea is best suited for an existing rancher, however, it can be adapted by anyone – ie.: by renting from a rancher. Thousands of cattle could be marketed this way. Such a project generates a lot of paperwork, thus, a computer program is essential.

A booking agent can become rich and famous and start with only an office and a telephone!

Select a catchy name, establish a rate card (10% is standard) and solicit clients. Prospects include entertainers, athletes and professional speakers. Obtain leads from any group or association of which they may be members.

Contact businesses such as cabarets and nightclubs, who employ singers and bands. The agency's challenge is then to secure lucrative engagements for its clients at these clubs.

To make a million dollars is not difficult. Buy one million chickens for one dollar each and sell them for two.

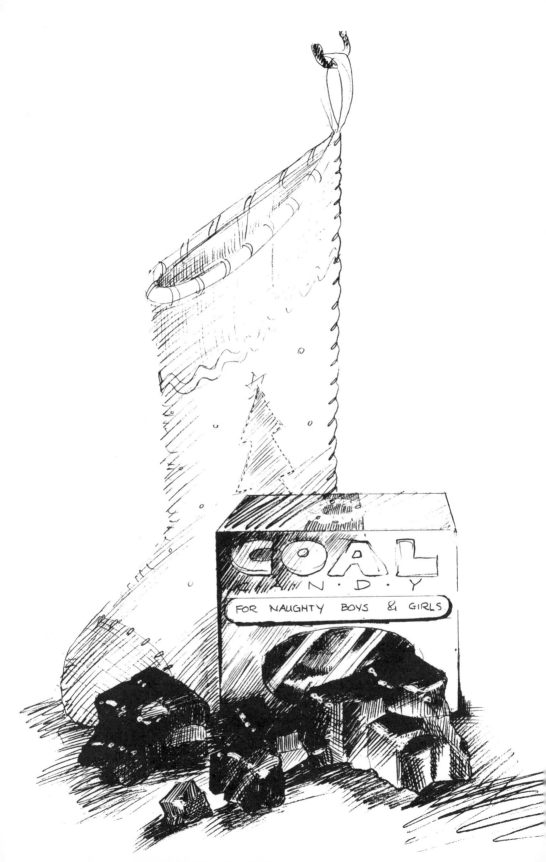

. . . he knows if you've been bad or good. . .

Traditionally, boys and girls who were naughty were threatened with having a piece of coal put into their Christmas stockings because they were undeserving of Santa's treats. Very often parents include a piece of coal in their children's stocking as a humorous gesture!

Product:
Christmas Coal Candy for naughty boys and girls. Coal Candy is a licorice flavored hard candy. The candy is black and when broken into chunk-like pieces, resembles coal. Each piece is uniquely different and is packaged in a clear bag. Each bag is packed in a colorful box with a traditional design depicting some aspect of Victorian mischief! The box has to be able to fit into a stocking.

Market:
This is a Christmas novelty item and would fall into the "stocking stuffer" category, retailing for under $5.00. It is a suitable gift to people of all ages — aren't we all naughty at some time or another?

(Continued on page 63)

Marketing Plan: The colorful boxes of candy would be displayed in a cardboard display stand, which is constructed out of the packaging material in which it is delivered. It would hold 72 boxes of candy. Coal Candy can be sold almost anywhere including department stores, convenience stores, gas bars, gift shops, candy stores, drug stores and grocery stores.

Since this is a seasonal impulse purchase, the packaging and point of purchase material is vital to its success.

Profit Potential: After the various costs associated with start-up, it is anticipated that with reasonable sales, the profit level would exceed $1.00 per box. It is also reasonable to assume that millions of units of this product could be merchandised.

Business Plan: This product is ideal for an existing candy manufacturer; however, a marketing firm can also be successful with this program by contracting the work out to existing manufacturers.

Fund Raising

Become an independent, professional fund raiser! Raise money for others for a fee (up to 25%) from the pledges and donations received. Prepare a brochure. Outline the commitments of time and energy that you are prepared to provide. Indicate that the fee will be a percentage and that it is negotiated to suit the situation. Note that your service will likely increase the amount of the funds raised. This increase, if achieved, will offset the cost.

Approach schools, churches and clubs, being careful to ensure they are credible charities. Fund raising can be very rewarding (financially too!).

Garden Plots

Here's a back to Mother Earth idea!

Most apartment and condo dwellers would like to have a garden of their own. Rent or buy a piece of farm land and divide off individual garden plots. Prepare a flyer or brochure with pictures and do mail drops at apartments within 45 minutes of the property. The owner or manager of a building could be very helpful distributing flyers and booking rentals. Rent out the garden plots by the month or by the season. A community crop of peas or carrots would be an added feature for the tenants. This seasonal venture can be profitable.

Prepare a resumé outlining your education and your business experiences. Prepare a brochure explaining why you should be consulted on a particular subject. Briefly review your strengths. Attach a rate card. Then place an advertisement in a newspaper:

Consultant For Hire

— Plumbing —

25 years experience in the trade. Office, sales and payroll knowledge. Ideally suited to assist emerging or new plumbing companies. Hourly rates, tax deductible. Please call Harry at (555) 555-5555.

Because it pays to buy expertise, all businesses can use a consultant at some time or another.

If your life is free of failure, you're not taking enough risks.

"Hi"
"Howdy"
"Congratulations!"

We've all sent messages like these by fax; and with more and more homes and offices being equipped with a fax, wouldn't it be nice to send a "Greet Sheet!" Unlike regular birthday, anniversary and Christmas cards which are folded, Greet Sheets would make a flat, easy-to-fax, greeting sheet.

The Greet Sheets could be planned and designed in the following categories:

Internal Office Memos:
- From the Desk of the Commander
- Great Idea!
- Well Done!
- I'm Sorry. . .
- Don't Forget
- Suggestion!
- You Are Invited

Business to Business:
- Please pay your bill
- Confidential
- Very Important / Take Note
- Announcement
- We apologize for the inconvenience
- New!

(Continued on page 71)

GREET SHEETS

GREET SHEETS
SEASONAL GREETINGS

GREET SHEETS
BUSINESS TO BUSINESS

GREET SHEETS
INTERNAL OFFICE MEMOS

GREET SHEETS
PERSONAL

- BIRTHDAYS
- WEDDINGS
- BON VOYAGE
- BIRTH ANNOUNCEMENT
- CONGRATULATIONS
- SYMPATHY

Business Greetings:

- Congratulations
- Thank You
- Good Luck on Your New Venture
- You are invited
- Well done
- Go for it!

Personal Greetings:

- Birthdays
- Bon Voyage
- Birth Announcement
- Wedding
- Sympathy
- Hi!
- Missing You
- Barmitzvah
- Graduation

Seasonal Greetings:

- Halloween
- Christmas
- Thanksgiving
- Valentine's Day
- Hanukkah
- Yom Kippur
- Easter
- St. Patrick's Day
- Happy New Year

(Continued on next page)

Specialty Business (Restaurant):

- Lunch Special
- Wine Tasting
- Dessert Special
- Free Coffee with Lunch
- Salad Special
- Cocktail Hour
- You have won a free dinner
- Discount
- Other

Greet Sheets could use a mix of humorous and serious greetings or two separate sheets for each division could be made.

Marketing: These could be designed in sets and packaged in a standard size file folder so that they are easy to store in a filing cabinet. Use pictures or illustrations wherever appropriate.

Each set could be sold separately or in a combined package for a special price. They could be retailed in the regular way or they could be marketed on a door to door basis during the summer, using the student workforce.

This idea is as broad as your imagination.

All that's needed is a video camera, cassettes, an invoice and a bank deposit book.

Approach businesses and residences offering to take pictures of their insurable contents; photographs are invaluable extra insurance in the event of theft or damage. For an additional fee, keep a second video on file in the event that the client's is lost or destroyed. Videos can be useful in establishing fair values for items in an insurance claim. Annual video updates can also be solicited. Written introductions and testimonials from well known individuals and companies will assist in securing contracts.

This idea is great for a one or two person team. However, it can also be greatly expanded. One or more persons could contract the work and organize a team of camera operators who would do the filming.

What matters is not the size of the dog in the fight, but the size of the fight in the dog.

For the colorful!

Artists often require the assistance of an independent experienced marketer to sell their work. There is art for every taste and taste for every art. Organize all available artists into a concentrated sales program. Charge each a set fee and a percentage of sales. Obtain a location and book the dates. Prepare, place and pay for an advertising campaign. Inform the press. Assist artists with pricing, sales plans and display set-up.

Example:

Expenses:

Rent a hall (or space in a mall) – 4 days	$ 600.00
Radio advertising – 4 days	500.00
Newspaper advertising – 4 days	500.00
Direct mailer/pamphlet advertising	500.00
Road signage/mail	400.00
Total	$2,500.00

Income:

Based on 10 artists:

$150.00 gallery fee x 10	$1,500.00
$20.00 per painting listing fee x 200	4,000.00
Admission @ $2 per person x 500	1,000.00
Gross Profit	$6,500.00
Less Costs	2,500.00
Net Profit	$4,000.00

Note: Additional financial considerations:
1) Charge a percentage fee for all sales.
2) Several shows per month can be done.

Making money at the top of the hill!

How many times has the very thought of loading and lugging your ski gear to the ski hill put you off a fun-packed day on the slopes? Or worse still – you're at home and you still have to pack your lunch and then lug it around the slopes when you get there! Imagine if each family had a large size locker to hold all their gear exclusively each season.

Here's how to do it!

Approach the management of the ski hill and secure one or more areas for lockers. These spots can be outside or preferably indoors in secure locations. Lockers could be constructed of wood, metal, or pre-formed plastic, with steel hardware. The intention is to provide a service and to make a profit.

Benefits:
- The ski hill benefits because it is ensured a steady captive clientele – they are unlikely to go anywhere else if their ski equipment is at a particular resort.

- Customers assured of security and convenience will ski more regularly.

- You benefit – you have a profitable business.

(Continued on next page)

Ski Lockers (continued)

Revenue (sample):

500 lockers @ $100.00 each		
($20.00 per month x 5 months)		$50,000.00
Cost @ $30.00 per unit		15,000.00
Profit		$35,000.00

Note: 1. The $15,000.00 used in the example is a one-time cost.
2. No provision has been made for any percentage of the funds paid to the ski hill or for the maintenance of the lockers.
3. Additional revenue is possible by retaining the rights to sell advertising for the sides, backs and fronts of the lockers. Potential advertisers include ski shops, ski manufacturers, restaurants, taxi companies and lock companies.

Funny Money

She thought he was one in a million, but actually he was won in a raffle!

Retailers, here's a way to help your community, customers and yourself! Establish a collection area for newspapers, bottles, cans and old clothes. Locate a spot in a store as far from the main entrance as possible so the customer must walk through the store twice.

Establish a refund or payment structure for each item and pay by way of a purchase credit. The credits can then be used only for purchases from that store. This system is similar in operation to frequent flyer programs where customers can accumulate points and use them when they want.

The customers have disposed of their bottles and papers and have used the money to purchase merchandise.

Merchants have increased their sales volume and although discounts are given by way of credits, they sell bottles and other items for additional revenue.

The environment too is a winner, as more people will collect and "get credit" for their recyclable items. A clean sweep!

This new idea, when developed, could revolutionize the retailing industry. This concept creates new markets for existing retail items. Merchandise is displayed by photographs via Storeboard signs and table top menus which should be distributed at no cost to taverns, lounges, motels and restaurants. The Storeboard allows these proprietors, who sell liquor, food and a few related items, the opportunity to supplement their profit by grossing nearly 100% in retail sales.

This exciting new concept could be developed along three formats:

1. Proshop for lounges and taverns
2. Storeshop for restaurants
3. Giftshop for motels

The Storeboard is a free-standing unit that could be made of plastic with a molded bottom. There are six or eight plexiglass slots on each panel. Photos of the merchandise are easily loaded into the slots.

The panels are designed to interlock, allowing as many as required to be placed side by side – depending on the location and availability of space.

The potential is incredible! The number of outlets or locations that qualify for Storeboards in North America are

Proshop: more than   100,000 locations
Storeshop: more than   700,000 locations
Giftshop: more than 1,000,000 locations

(Continued on page 83)

TAVERNS
More than 100,000 locations
qualify for a PROSHOP

RESTAURANTS
More than 700,000 locations
qualify for a STOREBOARD

Every location within these groups has staff on the payroll who can easily manage the retailing activities of Storeboards. Proprietors can diversify – selling brand name merchandise, without having increased taxes, labor, or building costs. They can only increase their sales and profits.

Storeboards should be able to merchandise brand name items for considerably less cost than department or discount stores due to low overhead. Volume buying also contributes to lower retail prices.

Potential Items:

Proshop (Bars):

- Sweatshirts
- T-shirts
- Sport T-shirts
- Baseball Caps
- Darts
- Pool Cues
- Billiards Rule Books
- Golf Paraphernalia
- Mini Hockey Sticks
- Billiard Gloves
- Beer Holsters
- Cue Stands
- Cue Cases
- Sunglasses
- Key Chains
- Board Games

Storeshop (Restaurants):

- Cookbooks
- Ball Caps
- Collectible Coffee Mugs
- T-shirts
- Music Cassette Tapes
- Computer Cartridges
- Comics
- Hardcover Books
- Video Movies
- Toys

Giftshop (Motels):

- Jewellery
- Souvenirs
- Gift Spoons
- Cameras / Film
- Perfume
- Electric Razors
- City History Books & Maps

(Continued on page 85)

MOTELS
More than 1,000,000 locations
qualify for a Gift Shop

Pre Pak

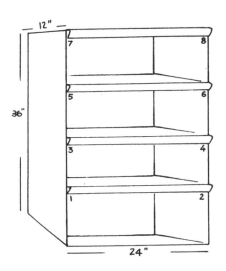

Menus have been designed for table top use in restaurants, taverns and lounges. The Menu offerings correspond with the Pre Pak products.

Inventory Control:　The Pre Pak has been designed to control merchandise for the retailer by serving as an organizer and a space saver. Pre Paks are made of durable cardboard and have up to six shelves.

There are to be corresponding numbers on the Storeboards and Pre Paks: ie.: an item pictured on the Storeboard is number 4, allowing the waiter to get the item from number 4 in the Pre Pak and deliver it to the customer.

Distribution:　Consider awarding exclusive distribution rights to specific territories. The cost could be up to $10,000.00 per territory. Approximately 100 territories could be available in North America.

Successful sales of the specific distribution territories would generate a large amount of capital that could be used for buying inventory. This tactic ensures a committed and dedicated sales force. One person should be able to place up to one dozen Storeboards daily. This figure multiplied by five week days and then by the number of territories, produces attractive returns.

(Continued on next page)

Storeboards (continued)

Territories: North America could be divided into 100
                  or more territories and sold if desired.
                  Demographics need to be thoroughly
                  analyzed in order to have efficient divi-
                  sion into geographical territories.

Sales Procedure: Dealers purchase all merchandise
                  exclusively from Storeboards. In return,
                  dealers are supplied with sales aids.
                  They establish accounts and service
                  them. The distribution agreement states
                  the exclusivity of product purchases, the
                  sales methods and the various controls
                  that exist.

Conclusion: Storeboards is an exciting idea!
                  Although described for big business,
                  Storeboards can be developed suc-
                  cessfully at any level. There are similari-
                  ties between vending machines and
                  Storeboards. One obvious difference is
                  that items of any size could be sold by
                  Storeboards! To be able to display
                  merchandise by pictures and also to be
                  able to deliver them to the customer in
                  this manner, is truly a big step forward
                  in retailing.

"Tie one on!"

With neck ties making a colorful entry back onto the fashion scene, here is a project that is fun and quick to be in and out of.

Contact a tie manufacturer and get a price on having custom designed ties made. Find out about the availability of sub-contracting. Next you would need to find a good artist/designer and get a quote for the design work. With these quotes in hand, add shipping, handling and your level of profit, then calculate the price per tie.

Let's say you market to car salesmen; you have your artist draw up the design in color, make up a package which you present to all the car dealerships and solicit your orders. Car dealers would then distribute them as gifts to their clients. Sell 1,000 car ties to the car dealership (directly or to their 10 salespeople). If your cost was $3.00 per tie and you sell for $5.00 per tie – you could make $2,000.00 in one day. You are happy – your clients are too, as it is tasteful advertising – the customer is happy and, who knows – he might just buy another car because of it.

Real estate firms, doctors, shoe retailers and colleges are other interesting markets.

Many businesses throughout the developed world, from time to time, consider investing in or expanding to foreign countries. However, few actually make investments due to restrictions of time and lack of knowledge of the countries and their politics.

A great opportunity for a foreign consulting firm! Such a firm would also act as a purchasing agent for its clients.

Advertise your services in selected newspapers in several countries. Target various sizes of enterprises. For example, a small printing company in Germany could purchase shares in a similar firm in New York.

Charge a set fee and a commission based on the values of the assets purchased. Several clients in several countries can be contracted at the same time. Include travel costs and other expenses in the fee structure. A minimum duration of three months should be contracted to allow time for becoming familiar with the clients and their requirements.

Clients are in the position of having an exclusive agent to represent their expansion interest. Firms will appreciate the opportunities to explore potential foreign investments.

Possible Names: Global Investment Agency
                    World Consultant Group

Strength in numbers! Investment Clubs are a complement to any type of individual regardless of experience or vocation.

Form an Investment Club with up to twelve members. By consensus, select a club name and set out the policies, rules and investment requirements of the club – very important so that disagreements within the club can be avoided when it is operational. The type of portfolios must be established at the beginning, ie.: stocks, and/or real estate. Each Investment Club member contributes a pre-set amount of money each month, which is invested as agreed on by the club.

An agenda should be followed and minutes kept. Proposed purchases are to be put forward as motions that are debated and voted on by the membership. Members chosen in rotation should be responsible for obtaining information on investments and distributing it to fellow members for analysis when they look to select, for example, a stock. The club should look for companies with growth potential, low debt, a low price-to-earnings ratio, and good management. There are Investment Club Associations in most cities. Contact some for further information which likely will include written manuals, suggested by-laws, a sample annual report and other organizational guides.

Investment Clubs are for everyone! The association with others in the group is important but the profit potential is the main incentive. Suggestions for contributions and descriptions are:

(Continued on next page)

Investment Club (continued)

Type of Investor	Description	Amount
Novice:	• Homemakers • Students, • Non-business background	$25-$100.00 per month
Regular:	• Office workers • Recent graduates	$100-$200.00 per month
Successful:	• Business owners • Sales representatives	$200-$500.00 per month
Sophisticated:	• Very successful business people	$500-$5,000.00 per month

The amount of purchase power and the increased potential for profit are relative to the contributions. Investment Clubs are for everyone!

To make your money dreams come true, you have to stay awake.

Egg Carton and Popsicle Sticks

Here is a crafty idea for juniors! Organize a group of friends and students. Collect and record the many suggested uses for egg cartons and popsicle sticks. Compile them in book form (made with a parent's or school's computer). Secure sponsorship, if possible, from a local box or egg company and sell the book.

Design the book for children and sell it at craft fairs, churches and schools.

The uses for egg cartons include everything from planters, pencil holders, robots to fire trucks. Buildings and vehicles can be made from popsicle sticks.

Take pictures or do drawings or some examples and include them in the book. A creative group of children will come up with hundreds of applications for both egg cartons and popsicle sticks! Other children enjoy the organized collection of these uses.

Possible Names: Toy Book
                    Egg Stick

There was a time when something you got for nothing didn't cost so much.

Drive Buy

Time is valuable. If you can offer a service that will save people time, you'll have a line-up!

It started back in the 50's and 60's with the drive-through restaurant. . . what a success!

Drive-through banks and fast-food outlets are now common-place and very convenient; however, there are very few other drive-through services available.

Imagine the driver about to hit a multi-lane highway heading south, knowing he'll be on the road at least 45 to 60 minutes. What does he need? A drink, newspaper, cigarettes, candy or milk his wife wanted him to buy on the way home. Most cities don't allow parking or stopping in the downtown area during peak traffic hours. The answer — a drive-through corner store!

What about a. . .

- drive-through smoke shop
- drive-through snack bar
- drive-through cappuccino bar
- drive-through laundry service
    (drop off a.m./pick up p.m.)
- drive-through photograph service
- drive-through newspaper & magazine stand
- drive-through grocery store
- drive-through bakery

This idea will get mileage!

VE THROUGH . . .
DRIVE THROUGH . . .
DRIVE THROUGH . . .
DRIVE THROUGH
OKE SHOP
DRY-CLEANER
Photo
COFFE
• CANDY
• CIGARETTES
• NEWSPAPERS
IN - A.M.
OUT - P.M.
Same day

All kids love surprises. Develop this idea and they'll get a surprise each time they buy a treat!

Lucky Packets are brightly decorated packets, each filled with a small amount of candy and a toy. Because children can't see into the packets before they open them, they are guaranteed a surprise each time.

Marketing:
Lucky Packets should be sold for a dollar or less so that they are affordable to young children.

Because this item is an impulse pur-chase, it is a perfect item for marketing at the point of purchase, (near the till or check-out counter). They can be dis-played on racks or spikes to create a colorful column of Lucky Packets. To enhance sales, make the toy part of a series of toys or part of a collection. Another idea would be to use a collector series of wildlife or sports cards with the toy and candy.

Suggestions:
- Separate packets could be developed for boys and girls to make the selec-tion of toys easier. Try pink packets for girls and blue ones for boys.
- Candied popcorn could be used instead of candy.

(Continued on next page)

Lucky Packets (continued)

- Once successful, a more expensive line and less expensive line could be developed, with the "better" packets having a more substantial surprise.
- Gifts should always be of equal value to prevent consumer resistance and disappointments.

This idea could prove to be lucky for you!

Senior Employment

Often senior citizens want to work at full or part-time jobs. In spite of their advanced years, they still wish to be involved and they often require the income.

Establish an agency for matching seniors to employers. Obtain a fee from one or both sides of the transaction. Advertise in newspapers and make personal contact with selected companies and at centers where seniors meet for recreation or fellowship. Design information forms and brochures for both the employee and employer.

Powdered Eggs In A Shell

Homemakers often find themselves out of eggs just when they are in the middle of making a cake.

Powdered eggs should be in every kitchen for just such a time. The shelf life for this product is almost limitless.

Package the egg powder equivalent of one egg in a plastic egg container. Plastic egg shells are available at specialty stores and wholesalers. Design egg cartons for a half-dozen and a dozen eggs; design a logo and select a slogan for the package. Present your product to supermarkets and food stores.

Now the homemaker can buy powdered eggs (or rather a unique package with powdered eggs in it).

Don't be chicken about making money. . . this is no yoke!

Money does talk. . . mine just said good-bye.

So you missed front row seats for the concert!. . . you only made it to the top of the stand for the game. . . and for $50.00 a ticket, you probably would have seen it better on T.V.! But then you miss the excitement of being there. Wait a minute! Why hasn't someone thought of this yet! Binoculars!

Install binoculars at all stadiums chained to backs or under-sides of seats. They would have to be very robust to withstand constant use and weather. They would be coin operated, either at the release mechanism, or have a timing mechanism which would enable the user to pay for pre-set periods of viewing.

It's possible that a company who manufactures binoculars would co-venture this service as it would be able to have its name on all binoculars installed at the stadium or theatre.

So, don't miss the game. . . get your sights set on this one!

Possible Names: I.C. Entertainment Co.
                    For Your Eyes Only

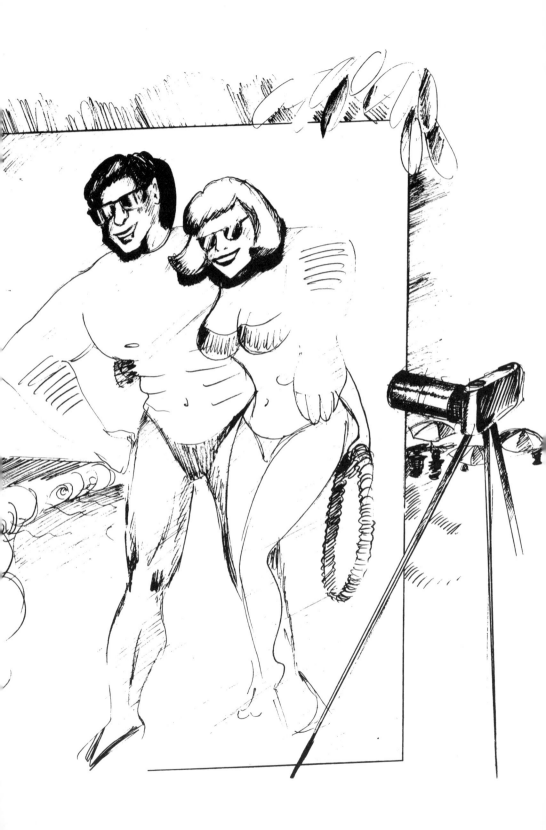

Beach Photographer

Many people long to have their pictures taken with someone famous.

Set up a photo booth at the beach. Make life-sized painted figures of famous people, luscious blondes, handsome hunks, etc., which are portable and free-standing. Take pictures of people standing next to the figures. In addition, have figures with cut-outs for their faces. Your clients would then peep through the cut-out and take on a new form!

Clients should pay for the photography up-front. Photographs can either be mailed to home addresses or collected at the booth, the same day if possible.

This idea is great for a summer job and is perfect for a student with an artistic flair and a good camera.

Beach Business

Locate a popular beach and set up a day rental business. Rent out lawn chairs, canoes, balls, floats and other beach-related items.

To avoid the start-up costs, approach a firm which is presently involved in these types of rentals and sub-lease the items from them. Snack food items could also be added.

Although seasonal, this could be quickly expanded by setting up additional outlets at other beaches.

This bright idea is secure!

Develop an enclosed storage locker with an attached covered area. The locker size should be 12' wide by 8' long; the height depends on the length and the use to be made of the outside area. Two suggestions for sizes are:

    1. R.V. (Recreational Vehicle) style: 10' x 40' total (32' out and 8' enclosed) x 12' high.

    2. Regular: 10' x 28' (20' out and 8' enclosed) x 8' high.

Locate a small piece of property close to a lake or other types of recreational sites. Buy or lease it. Advertise rentals by sending brochures to selected boat and R.V. owners.

Build the units as required. Costs will vary depending on locations. Blacktop, power and other services may not be necessary and could possibly be avoided. Build large doors on the locker so renters can store motorcycles, snowmobiles and other large items.

This facility is very functional and effective. The development can be easy. The return on investment can be significant. Offer rental discounts for pre-payments on long-term leases to complement the cash flow.

Commission Sales Structure

The inter-workings of salespeople at the same company often do not benefit their company, customers or themselves. An idea to improve this is to pool the resources of the salespeople.

Sales Commission: For example, if the salespeople at an automobile dealership pooled their earnings, the mad rush to reach the clients entering the building would stop. Customers are able to view the various vehicles unpressured before being approached. Sales personnel agree to respond to the demands of each other's customers. The sales team is effective and efficient. The dealership benefits through increased sales and customer satisfaction.

Customer Public
Relations:

A percentage of all commissions should be put into a public relations fund. Customers receive a gift each for the next three to five years since it is anticipated that they will purchase another vehicle within that time. The gift in the $10.00 range has an enclosed card, stating, "Please let us sell you your next vehicle." One example of a gift is a wrist watch with the auto dealership's name on the face, along with a message like, "We have time for you. . . please let us sell you a car." This is great planning for the next sale. Approach the dealership for assistance in the funding for the program.

Summary: This structure can be very effective. However before it is used, various policies and rules must be outlined. It is recommended that an accountant and a business planner be consulted to assist with details and with the general plan.

Work Agent

A real freelancer! Search for jobs that need doing, homes that need painting, siding, roof repairs, yard work or for vehicles that have dents or bad tires.

Record the addresses and names of the people and even photos of the items if possible. Have identification prepared for your auto and yourself to avoid being mistaken for a robber "casing" the area. Contact the appropriate businesses who normally work with these situations and sell them the list of the people needing this type of service. Negotiate a flat fee plus a percentage of the sales. What a great prospect list!

Tin cans, labels and possibly a label printer are needed for this idea. The product is a timed message, a novel gift idea. For example, several months before his wife's birthday a man puts a bracelet and a note in a can. . . you seal, print and label it. . . he presents it to his wife. The label would boldly state: Do not open until your birthday! The can is a novelty and is quite a conversation piece for the next several months while the can is displayed in their home.

This concept could be operated within an existing business or done independently. It would be best suited for a mall location where there is a lot of pedestrian traffic.

Prepare the necessary paperwork and do the research. Proper signage is required.

Short-term joke items and long-term messages are both appealing, ie.: sealed ten year anniversary messages would be great to give out at weddings. Parents' special thoughts for their child at birth could be sealed until the child's 21st birthday. The ideas are endless!

Whoever said money can't buy happiness hasn't done much shopping.

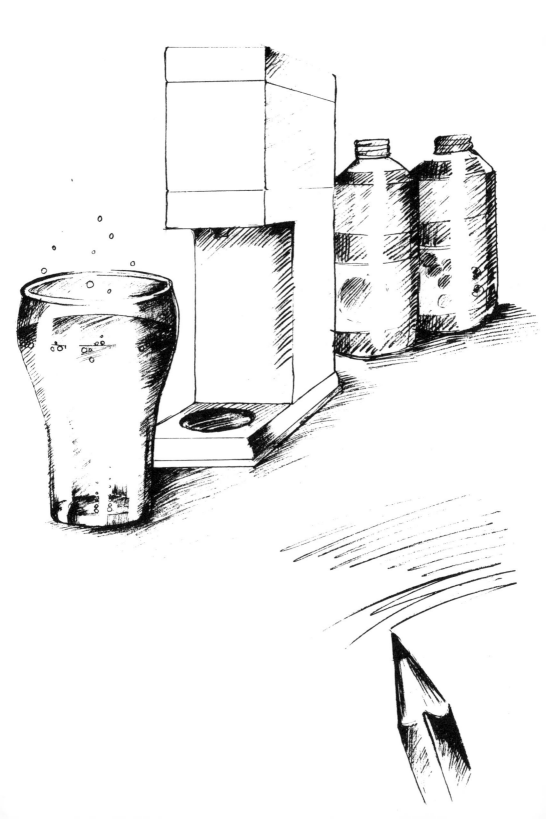

Every home should have one!

With all the problems and inconveniences (shelf space, environment and cost) caused by the cans and bottles from bottled pop, it is surprising that not many homes in North America have their own soda maker. In a number of other countries, soda makers are as common on the countertop as coffee makers!

This is great! All you need to do is take a glass of cold water, pour it into the soda maker, press a release button which forces carbon dioxide into the water, then pour it out, add flavored syrup and you have soda pop! There are a number of these soda makers on the market in countries such as Sweden, Australia and South Africa. These soda makers could be used or one could be designed that would meet the tastes and requirements of people in North America.

The Market: Every home in North America.

The Products:
- A soda maker approximately the size of a coffee maker (requires no electricity).
- Pressurized carbon dioxide cylinders (housed inside the soda maker).
- The syrups – there is a broad spectrum of flavored syrups.

(Continued on page 115)

- Re-usable and sealable bottles for storing soda water or soda pop in the refrigerator.
- Plastic pump bottles – used for storing syrups and capable of dispensing a pre-measured amount of syrup into each glass.

Marketing:

This product would be suitable for a large corporation with an established network of retail outlets or for a start-up enterprise.

Market it to the public through retail outlets. Set up a stall at each location, demonstrating the product and offering the public the opportunity to taste the pop. Units are sold on site. It's at this point that the diversity of this product becomes exciting. Now that everyone has a soda maker, they will need. . .

- Gas cylinders to be re-filled: This is done by the customer returning an empty cylinder in exchange for a full one and paying a fee only for the re-fill. Empty cylinders are safety checked, re-filled, sealed and ready for the next use.

(Continued on next page)

• Syrups: Consumer demand will result in syrups eventually being available at grocery stores.

• Accessories: These include the dispensing bottles, the re-usable refrigerator bottles and other useful items that will be developed by the company as it develops the product and its market.

Possible Names.:   Pop's Home
                    Soda Still

This idea has a lot of sparkle!

Even if you're on the right track, you'll get run over if you just sit there.

Real estate sales commission is a large expense when a property is sold. Residential rates are often 6 to 7% of the first $100,000.00 of the sale price. The percentage on the balance of the sale price is usually reduced. Effectively, a realtor is your employee. If your house takes two months to sell and the commission is $10,000.00, then you have employed the realtor for $5,000.00 a month. Not bad when you consider that rarely does a vendor know the background or qualifications of the salesperson. Most often the fees are not negotiated and a detailed marketing program for the property is not obtained.

Here is a wonderful opportunity for a middle person to work between realtors and vendors. Start a Listing Service company. Prepare a plan and advertise this service in newspapers and through accounting and legal firms. Secure a fee in the $100.00 to $300.00 range from those wishing to sell their property. Take photos and prepare a listing package on the property. Forward to every realtor in the area requesting that they bid on the listing. Their submissions need to include:

- Commission rate
- Advertising plan
- Open House plan
- Experience
- Expectations and projections
- Background

(Continued on page 119)

Real Estate Listing Service (continued)

The Listing Service assembles the replies and presents them, along with a summary and recommendations, to the vendor. The vendor now is in the position of being able to properly choose an employee.

The Listing Service is considered to be a consulting, advertising or clearing company. Revenues can be obtained from each party, a fee from the vendor and a fee from the realtor. The realtor's amount is made up of a bid fee plus a referral or consulting fee based on the commission rate earned. Consideration should be given to providing this service at no cost to the vendors, thereby encouraging their use of the service.

Possible Names are: National Listing Service
American Listing Service
Property Listing Service

Listing Services have the potential to change the real estate business as we know it. This method can make the selling of real estate very competitive and more efficient. Finally real estate sales can be more competitive through an organized and concentrated bid market.

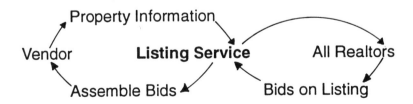

Property Information

Vendor   **Listing Service**   All Realtors

Assemble Bids   Bids on Listing

Pedal to profit! There are more cyclists and bike owners than ever before. Whole families and groups are biking together.

Athletes, fitness cyclists and pleasure riders have caused huge demands in the area of bike sales and service. Conspicuous by its absence is the Bike Wash! Develop a single Bike Wash or even a national chain of them.

Sub-leasing an area from an existing car wash is the most economical method but a start-up enterprise would also work well.

Design narrow wash bays separated by spray walls. Include stands or holders in the bays for bike helmets so that clients can clean them at the same time.

Signage and a detailed description of the venture are important. The bike owners must know that the wash is exclusively for their use. Tell them of the advantages of using a Bike Wash; protecting their investment by steam cleaning old grease and chain oil and by steam washing to prolong bicycle life and protect the paint job.

(Continued on next page)

Bike Wash (continued)

Accessories for sale could include:

- Helmets
- Helmet covers
- Velcro money holders for bikes
- Air pumps
- Chain oil
- Wrench sets

In addition, the Bike Wash, by selling snack items, becomes a gathering place for bike owners.

Possible Names: Cycle Cleaner
                    Two Wheel Wash

A cynic knows the price of everything and the value of nothing.

Yes, you do have to be silent in the library. . . however, that doesn't mean you can't make money there!

This idea is an all-around winner. Help the library, help protect the books, help your sponsors and help yourself.

Approach librarians, offering them free plastic book jackets for their books. Determine the type of covers they use and the sizes. Then find a sponsor – one large company or a number of smaller ones. Have them pay a fee to have their advertising placed on the plastic jackets. The fee should be sufficient to cover the cost of designing and producing the jackets as well as having them printed. Also included in that amount, factor in your profit. All that remains to be done is to deliver the jackets to the library and then see them in use!

Suggestions:

- Keep the advertising small and tasteful so that it isn't offensive.

- No doubt the librarian will receive complaints from certain sectors who felt they weren't given the opportunity to participate in the advertising program. Good – remember that plastic covers wear out and get ripped, the library also is continually purchasing new books that will need additional covers. Have the librarian keep names of interested sponsors and be sure to contact them promptly.

(Continued on page 125)

- If this venture proves profitable for you, it may be a good idea to make a cash donation to the library for the purchase of new books or offer the library a percentage of the sponsorship money – this will keep the librarian happily "feeding" your business.

Now you can judge a book by its cover!

Ever feel like a donut? You're either in the dough or in the hole.

Sombrero

Two popular snack food items are ice cream and donuts. In addition to specialty stores in each of these areas, many restaurants and cafés sell these products. Combine the two . . . one or more scoops of ice cream placed in the center of a warm donut and you have. . . a Sombrero! Soft ice cream or yogurt can also be used. A new product from old products and new flair.

This idea has great potential! Use as an addition to your menu or build a store (or a chain of stores!) around the product. This would compete with existing ice cream parlors and donut shops. Design a store with a Mexican theme and use Sombreros throughout.

Possible Names: Sombrero's
                    Top Hat
                    Donut Tops

"A worker who spends most of the time watching the clock usually remains one of the hands."

Concept:	Vertical blinds are very popular and usually they are color coordinated to fit the room decor. Although they are attractive, when closed they are boring! Pictures, designs, logos and other scenes can easily be painted on blinds. Open, blinds appear "normal" but when they are closed. . . Art! Finally. . . a way to "move a room!"
Market:	Millions of vertical blinds are in use in homes, offices, hospitals, and government buildings. In addition to the present market, there is the follow-up market of change, ie.: after several months sell a new picture to an old customer.
Program:	• Research the best design application method. • Design a marketing package (also offer to do custom design work). • Design a price and service package. • Solicit businesses and home owners for business.

(Continued on page 131)

Potential:

The assumption is that a lot of money can be earned. The market is huge and the idea is exciting! Independent owners could easily have several artists working for them. Blind Designs can be as large as your imagination.

The company logo or art can be put on the reverse side so that designs are also visible from the exterior.

Possible Names:

Change Your Outlook
Blind Ideas
Blind Art
Vertical Blind Fashion
Window Art Design

NEED A JOB?
NEED A WORKER?
"HIRE OR SEEK"
TO PLACE AN ADVERTISEMENT
pay a minimum charge on
1-900
TO RETRIEVE AN ADVERTISEMENT
call free on
1-800

Many established companies are taking advantage of the cost-effective and broad networking possibilities of the pay-to-call, 1-900 service. The credibility of some of these companies has added strength and a new dimension to what was previously a limited market. A wealth of information is now available using a 1-900 service – everything from sports and weather information to advice from a veterinary surgeon!

With unemployment rates at extremely high levels in parts of North America and with the cry for help equally loud in other areas, this idea brings them together – nationally and also possibly internationally.

"Hire and Seek" is an employment service offered on a national basis via both the 1-900 and 1-800 services.

If you were placing an ad in a national newspaper either to offer or seek employment, do you have any idea what it would cost? A lot! By dialing 1-900, you place your ad, pay a set amount and then have it run for a stipulated period, possibly two weeks.

During that period people wishing to listen to the ads would dial a 1-800 number and spend as long as they wanted on this free line to hear your message as well as other messages.

Everybody wins, people find help, people find work and the newly developed Hire and Seek company finds their bank balance has grown!

(Continued on next page)

Hire and Seek (continued)

A few tips. . .
- A 1-900 and 1-800 service is only as good as its advertising!
- When starting out it is best to take advantage of an established bureau as they have all the essential equipment set-up.

Your search for an interesting business could begin right here!

Idea Picture

Often messages or sayings are photocopied, passed around and put on bulletin boards. Soon the impact is lost with the message itself.

Take two messages or stories to get type-set, have them printed, put them into a two-sided frame and sell them to businesses. This product is ideal for door-to-door sales. If print and frames are of high quality, business people will display these profound messages forever!

Packaged properly, these will be purchased and displayed. In addition to adding character to a room, the messages constantly provoke thought and conversation.

One example of a story is:

The Hot Dog Story

A man lived by the side of the road and sold hot dogs.
He was hard of hearing so he had no radio.
He had trouble with his eyes so he read no newspapers.
But he sold good hot dogs.
He put up a sign on the highway telling how good they were.
He stood by the side of the road and cried, "Buy a hot dog, Mister."
And people bought.
He increased his meat and bun orders.
He bought a bigger stove to take care of his trade.
He got his son home from college to help him.
But then something happened. . .
His son said, "Father haven't you heard the news?
There's a big recession on.
The unemployment situation is terrible.
The energy situation is worse."
Whereupon the father thought, "Well, my son has been to college.
He reads the papers and he listens to the radio, and he ought to know."
So the father cut down on his meat and bun orders.
Took down his advertising signs.
And no longer bothered to stand on the highway to sell hot dogs.
And his hot dog sales fell almost overnight.
"You're right, son," the father said to the boy,
"We are certainly in the middle of a great recession."

Ice Pack Bandanna

A cool idea!

Enclose two artificial ice packs or water filled plastic holders in a brightly colored cloth. Obtain advertising for the ends which may be printed onto the fabric or attached. Market to runners, tennis players and other athletes. Running clubs and gyms are good places for sales prospects.

The Bandanna can be worn as a scarf and can be re-frozen for repeated use. This is a refreshing fashion idea.

Potential advertisers include health food stores, sports stores and beverage companies.

Bumper sticker on an elaborate motorhome: "We're spending our children's inheritance."

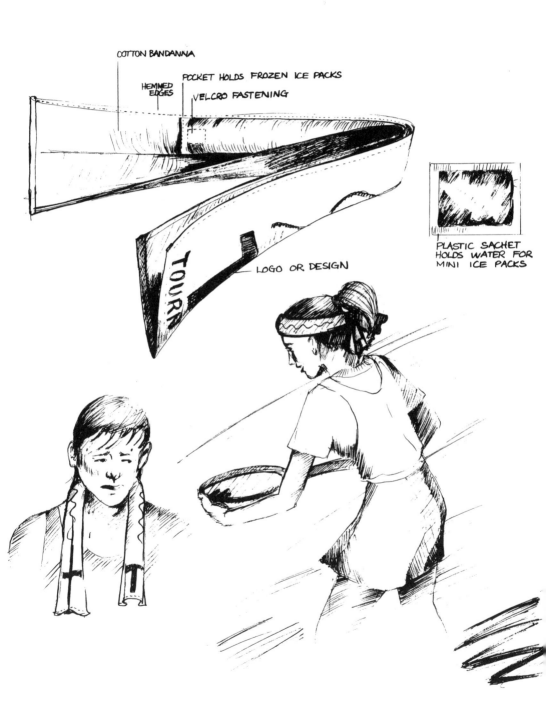

COTTON BANDANNA

HEMMED EDGES

POCKET HOLDS FROZEN ICE PACKS

VELCRO FASTENING

TOURN

LOGO OR DESIGN

PLASTIC SACHET HOLDS WATER FOR MINI ICE PACKS

Peoples Grocery Shopper

Shop 'till you drop! (and get paid for it).

Many people enjoy a fast lifestyle and lack the time to grocery shop. Often this results in empty cupboards and a restaurant diet.

Provide a grocery shopping and delivery service. Charge a flat rate, ie.: $5.00 and a percentage of the grocery bill.

When warranted by high volume buying, you could provide this service at no cost to the customer. The grocery store could pay your fee on a commission basis. The advantage to them would be the additional sales and repeat business.

Select a market area and advertise with door-to-door flyers. The format of the actual grocery list is extremely important. Prepare an extensive list and include illustrations of brand name products.

Encourage clients to utilize a fax machine. They then could fax a completed list when necessary.

Store owners are motivated to work with you as this concept can deliver large numbers of consumers from other market areas who would normally not travel any distance to their store. The idea has great potential, particularly in large urban centers.

Happy shopping!

	1KG	500G	Quantity
		✓	3
	✓		5
	✓		

Campbell's Soup
- TOMATO
- CHICKEN
- VEGETABLE
- BEEF

| | | ✓ | 2 |

Harvest Vegetables
	1KG	500G	QUANTITY
POTATOES		✓	5
CORN		✓	5
PEAS			
BEETS			
CARROTS			

Deerios Cereal
	1.5KG	750g	QUANTITY
REGULAR	✓		1
MALTED		✓	1
WITH OATBRAN			
NO SUGAR OR SALT			

Pops Cereal
ONE SIZE ONLY
- CHOCOLATE ✓
- HONEY
- FRUIT

Apartment Ranch Development

A real estate development with a difference!

Obtain property on which to build an apartment complex having several acres of extra land for the construction of horse paddocks, stalls and corrals.

Tenants of the apartments would be horse owners and would be assigned a particular stall and area for an additional amount of monthly rent, (ie.: apartment number 12 would also have horse stall number 12). Locate the property close to public areas that can easily be accessed for riding. Design the horse stalls with enclosed or attached tack rooms. The horse area is separated from the apartments with trees, shrubs and fences, designed in a courtyard style and including separate and common pasture areas.

A suggested site layout, based on a 16-unit apartment complex, is provided.

It is best to sell to people rather than wait for them to buy.

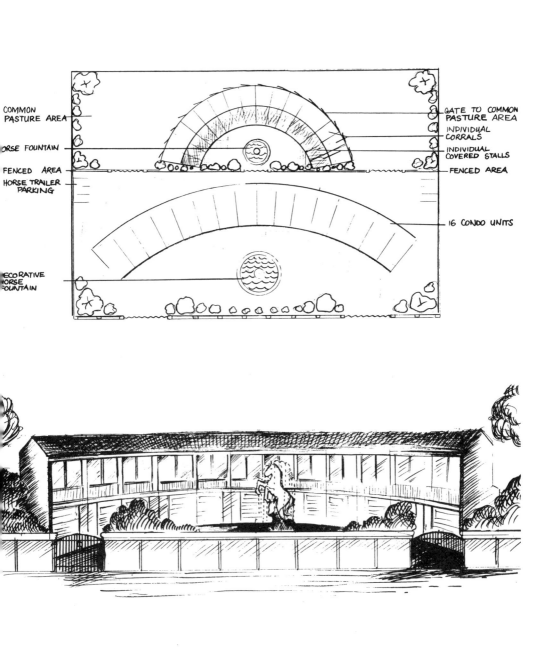

COMMON PASTURE AREA

ORSE FOUNTAIN

FENCED AREA

HORSE TRAILER PARKING

ECO RATIVE ORSE OUNTAIN

GATE TO COMMON PASTURE AREA

INDIVIDUAL CORRALS

INDIVIDUAL COVERED STALLS

FENCED AREA

16 CONDO UNITS

Cappuccino Billiard Shop

Pool. . . right on cue!

Billiards, commonly known as pool, is a great game which can become a favorite for all ages.

The idea is to combine pool with a cappuccino and pro shop business. Each of these are good stand-alone businesses and as a group present a fantastic opportunity.

Locate a high traffic location on ground level with ample parking. Investigate the availability of sufficient yard and exterior signage. About 5,000 sq. ft. is needed to accommodate 20 pool tables. A further 1,000 sq. ft. more or less is jointly needed for the cappuccino bar and pro shop.

Pool: Windows are important to help create an open and bright atmosphere. Design a non-smoking section for some of the pool tables. Target business people, families and students for mid-day games (a new fun "meeting room"). Contact billiard supply companies for help in budgeting and equipment purchases. Charge by the hour. Rent pool cues. Consider selling long-term leases on enclosed storage racks for pool cue owners. Establish leagues. Promote professional games.

Cappuccino Bar: This should have a separate entrance to attract non-pool players. Design the

(Continued on page 144)

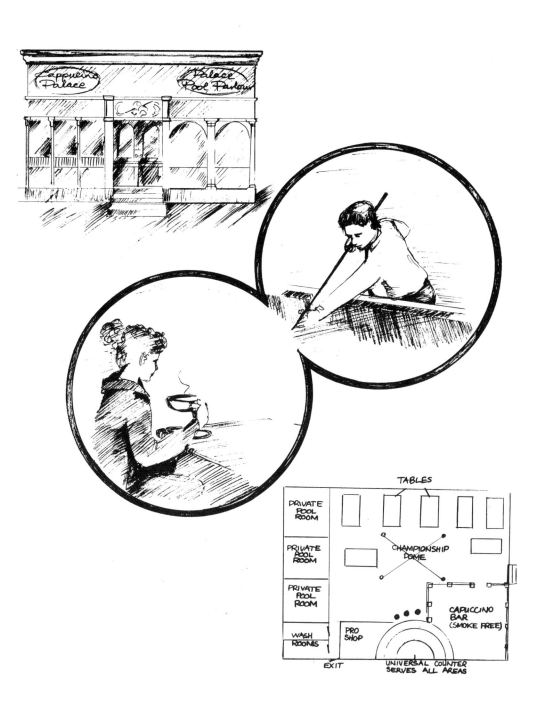

seating so the Cappuccino Bar can also serve the people playing pool and that the people in the café can observe the fun. Specialty coffees will be a big attraction to the customers and in turn they will be attracted to watching or playing pool.

Pro Shop:

A separate entrance as well as inside access would be good, as a non-pool market can be attracted to the store. Store customers must have unobstructed views of the games area. This highlights the difference of this pro shop. Items for sale are to include pool cues, shirts, shoes, golf equipment, sports videos and other sporting items.

Other:

Effectively, this idea is a mall-type atmosphere where each business benefits from the customer of the other. The anchor or main business is the pool room. Other businesses like a hair stylist, bridge club or an accounting office could also be included in this business mix. Although each business is connected, separate owners for each are possible.

Potential:
Pool rooms have recently surged in popularity and can be very profitable. This idea promotes a mix of trend businesses that could easily be packaged and reproduced throughout other areas if desired. Start-up costs are relatively low and projected pay backs can be measured in months. A detailed plan is required for each area as real estate and equipment costs vary. Liquor sales could also be considered.

Possible Names:
Palace Pool Parlor
Cappuccino Palace
Palace Pro Shop

The banker quit his job because he was bored. He lost interest in everything.

...ME — $000.00	LOGO — $000.00	SLOGAN — $00.00
Palace { OIL FARM CAPITAL INC VENTURES		"Royal Treatment" "Kings of Service" "We serve you"
Rock { INVESTMENTS DEVELOPMENTS CAPITAL OIL CO.		"Hard to beat" "Rock solid" "Built to stay"
Island { HOLIDAYS MARINE NURSERIES DEVELOPMENTS	Island	"Create your own paradise" "The sweet smell of success" "Experience the Island" "A weekend paradise"
Blue Bird { INVESTMENTS HOLIDAYS APARTMENTS SNACK CO.		bring happiness" holidays" from the sky" snacky"

Company Name Choice

Company Name Choice

Pick a name!

Collect and create names that can be used for new corporations. Prepare samples of slogans and logos that go with the names. Catalog each for sales presentations to prospective clients. Refer clients to a print shop for the printing of business cards, letterhead and stationery. Charge a fee to the printer.

Tens of thousands of businesses and individuals incorporate companies annually. Many struggle with selecting a name for their venture. When a name is chosen, often it or one similar, is already in use and unavailable. The next choice is often a compromise as few names are available to choose from.

Contact law firms and make them aware of this new service. Provide them with brochures and constantly update them with new names and logos. Prepare sections for various ventures like farming, oil, lumber and real estate businesses. Deal with as many law firms as possible and pay them a fee for their services. Provide an instruction page to outline the steps required, ie.: when a client of the law firm wishes to incorporate a company, present the book of names for their review. Once a name is selected, the name is to be removed from the list immediately, as others at different law firms are also viewing the names. The cost is billed by the law firm and can be forwarded after the appropriate fees are deducted.

(continued on next page)

Company Name Choice (continued)

Company names could sell for anywhere from $25.00 to $500.00 and logos for considerably more. Substantial numbers of both could be sold daily. Consider a smaller fee for a name if the client creates its own name from the contents of the name catalog. This would have to be monitored by the law firm.

Publications are available with names for new babies. . . why not for new companies!

Possible Names: Corporate Mug Book
                   Name That Business
                   Image Book

Too many committees waste hours and keep minutes.

Flower Power

People buy flowers at flower stores.. . . stores have rent, taxes, utilities, labor and inventory costs and competition. Become a Flower Broker. . . sell flowers to individuals and broker the sales to existing flower businesses.

Contact people by phone and obtain dates for when flowers are required, ie.: birthdays, anniversaries, etc. Encourage purchases for relatives or friends that normally would not receive flowers. Diarize these and contact the customer before each date to solicit a sale.

Sell the order to a flower shop who provides the flowers and does the delivery.

This is a telephone business and requires evening and weekend work. Customers will get to rely on this service and will no longer have to rush to do last minute flower shopping.

Computer Consultant

Small businesses and families often require assistance in these areas:
- The selection of an appropriate computer system.
- The set-up of the system.
- Housecall service to help with the computer.
- General advice regarding programs, costs and servicing.

Prepare brochures and contact computer retailers for leads. The yellow pages is a good place to advertise. Charge by the hour or by the job.

Notes

Notes

Notes

Notes

The author is available for business consulting and speaking engagements. If your organization, business or club would like more information, please include the name, phone and fax number of the contact person below with a brief outline of your interest to:

Bright Publishing Inc. Bright Publishing Inc.
Box 24002, Downtown P.O. Room 261, Box 5000
Kelowna, British Columbia Oroville, Washington
Canada V1Y 9P9 U.S.A. 98844

_____

_____

_____

_____

_____

_____

_____

_____

Any Bright Business Idea or money joke that you wish to share can be mailed to Bright Publishing Inc. at either of the above addresses.

If these are new to the publisher and used in future Bright Business Ideas publications, special acknowledgement will be given.

Bright Business Ideas

Bright Publishing Inc.
Box 24002, Downtown P.O.
Kelowna, British Columbia
Canada V1Y 9P9

Bright Publishing Inc.
Room 261, Box 5000
Oroville, Washington
U.S.A. 98844

Order a Bright Business Idea Book by Mail:

I would like to order the Bright Business Idea book(s):

_____ x $14.99 ea. + $2.00 per book = _____
Quantity   Amount   Postage &   Total Amount
                                  Handling   Enclosed

(please print)

Name:_____

Street:_____

City: _____

Prov./State:_____Postal/Zip:_____

* Please make check/cheque or money order payable to:
  Bright Publishing Inc.
• Canadian residents add G.S.T.
• Orders outside Canada to be paid in U.S. funds by check/cheque
  or money order.
• Prices subject to change without prior notice.
• No C.O.D.'s please.

Gift Card Message

We will gladly enclose your personal message with the book sent
as a gift. Write your message in the area provided below. Please
put name of receiver on the order card above.

A GIFT FOR YOU

**Bright
Business
Ideas**

Bright Business Ideas

Bright Publishing Inc.
Box 24002, Downtown P.O.
Kelowna, British Columbia
Canada V1Y 9P9

Bright Publishing Inc.
Room 261, Box 5000
Oroville, Washington
U.S.A. 98844

Order a Bright Business Idea Book by Mail:

I would like to order the Bright Business Idea book(s):

_____ x $14.99 ea. + $2.00 per book = _____
Quantity   Amount   Postage &   Total Amount
                                   Handling   Enclosed

(please print)

Name:_____

Street:_____

City: _____

Prov./State:_____Postal/Zip:_____

* Please make check/cheque or money order payable to:
  Bright Publishing Inc.
- Canadian residents add G.S.T.
- Orders outside Canada to be paid in U.S. funds by check/cheque
  or money order.
- Prices subject to change without prior notice.
- No C.O.D.'s please.

_____

Gift Card Message

We will gladly enclose your personal message with the book sent as a gift. Write your message in the area provided below. Please put name of receiver on the order card above.

A GIFT FOR YOU
Bright
Business
Ideas